NATIONAL GEOGRAPHIC
School Publishing

T0058636

Cómo se mueven los animales

Ricardo Lopez

PICTURE CREDITS
Illustrations by Trish Hart (4–5, 14–15).
Cover, 1, 2, 6 (above left, below left & above right), 7 (above left & below right), 9 (above right), 11 (all), 12 (all), 13 (above left & below right), 16 (above right, center right, below left & below right), Getty Images; 6 (below right), 8 (left & below right), 9 (below), 10 (below right), 13 (above right), 16 (above left, center left & center), Photolibrary.com; 7 (above right), 8 (above right), 10 (above right), Dave Watts/naturepl.com; 9 (above left), 10 (above left), APL/Corbis.

Produced through the worldwide resources of the National Geographic Society, John M. Fahey, Jr., President and Chief Executive Officer; Gilbert M. Grosvenor, Chairman of the Board.

PREPARED BY NATIONAL GEOGRAPHIC SCHOOL PUBLISHING
Ericka Markman, Senior Vice President and President Children's Books and Education Publishing Group; Steve Mico, Senior Vice President and Publisher; Marianne Hiland, Editorial Director; Lynnette Brent, Executive Editor; Michael Murphy and Barbara Wood, Senior Editors; Bea Jackson, Design Director; David Dumo, Art Director; Margaret Sidlowsky, Illustrations Director; Matt Wascavage, Manager of Publishing Services; Sean Philpotts, Production Manager.

SPANISH LANGUAGE VERSION PREPARED BY NATIONAL GEOGRAPHIC SCHOOL PUBLISHING GROUP
Sheron Long, CEO; Sam Gesumaria, President; Fran Downey, Vice President and Publisher; Margaret Sidlosky, Director of Design and Illustrations; Paul Osborn, Senior Editor; Sean Philpotts, Project Manager; Lisa Pergolizzi, Production Manager.

MANUFACTURING AND QUALITY MANAGEMENT
Christopher A. Liedel, Chief Financial Officer; Phillip L. Schlosser, Director; Clifton M. Brown III, Manager.

BOOK DEVELOPMENT
Ibis for Kids Australia Pty Limited.

SPANISH LANGUAGE TRANSLATION
Tatiana Acosta/Guillermo Gutiérrez

SPANISH LANGUAGE BOOK DEVELOPMENT
Navta Associates, Inc.

Published by the National Geographic Society
Washington, D.C. 20036-4688

Copyright © 2008 National Geographic Society. All rights reserved.
Reproduction of the whole or any part of the contents without written permission from the publisher is prohibited. National Geographic, National Geographic School Publishing, National Geographic Windows on Literacy and the Yellow Border are registered trademarks of the National Geographic Society.

ISBN: 978-0-7362-3828-1

Printed in Mexico
Print Number: 05 Print Year: 2023

Contenido

Pensar y conversar	4
¿Cómo se mueven los animales?	6
Caminar	7
Trepar	8
Correr	9
Brincar	10
Nadar	11
Arrastrarse	12
Volar	13
Usar lo que aprendieron	14
Glosario ilustrado	16

Pensar y conversar

¿Qué animales ven en la charca? ¿Cómo se mueven?

¿Cómo se mueven los animales?

Los animales se mueven de diferentes maneras.

Caminar

Algunos animales pueden **caminar.**

Un pato puede caminar.

Un elefante puede caminar.

Un oso puede caminar.

Trepar

Algunos animales pueden **trepar.**

Un oso puede trepar.

Una cabra puede trepar.

Un gato puede trepar.

Correr

Algunos animales pueden **correr.**

Un gato puede correr.

Un ciervo puede correr.

Un conejo puede correr.

Brincar

Algunos animales pueden **brincar.**

Un conejo puede brincar.

Un canguro puede brincar.

Una rana puede brincar.

Nadar

Algunos animales pueden **nadar.**

Una rana puede nadar.

Un pez puede nadar.

Una tortuga puede nadar.

Arrastrarse

Algunos animales pueden **arrastrarse.**

Un cangrejo puede arrastrarse.

Una tortuga puede arrastrarse.

Una mariquita puede arrastrarse.

Volar

Algunos animales pueden **volar.**

Una mariquita puede volar.

Un guacamayo puede volar.

Un pato puede volar.

Usar lo que aprendieron

¿Qué animales ven en el parque? ¿Cómo se mueven?

arrastrarse

brincar

caminar

correr

moverse

nadar

trepar

volar

Glosario ilustrado

arrastrarse

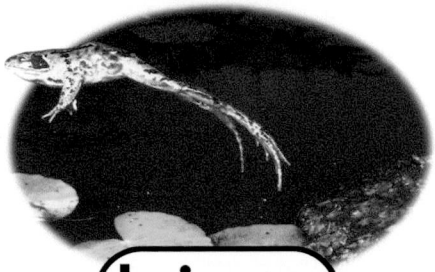

brincar

caminar

correr

nadar

trepar

volar